GUIDE TO GHOSTS AND HAUNTINGS

Ghost Hunters

Carla Mooney

San Diego, CA

About the Author

Carla Mooney is the author of many books for young adults and children. She lives in Pittsburgh, Pennsylvania, with her husband and three children.

© 2025 ReferencePoint Press, Inc.
Printed in the United States

For more information, contact:
ReferencePoint Press, Inc.
PO Box 27779
San Diego, CA 92198
www.ReferencePointPress.com

ALL RIGHTS RESERVED.
No part of this work covered by the copyright hereon may be reproduced or used in any form or by any means—graphic, electronic, or mechanical, including photocopying, recording, taping, web distribution, or information storage retrieval systems—without the written permission of the publisher.

Picture Credits:
Cover: Jorac/Shutterstock
 6: James Leynse/SCI FI Channel
10: Fototeca Gilardi/Bridgeman Images
12: The Print Collector/Alamy Stock Photo
17: Associated Press
21: Gwoweii/Shutterstock
23: ZUMA Press Inc/Alamy Stock Photo
26: Juiced Up Media/Shutterstock
31: SamuelBartlett/Shutterstock
35: ZUMA Press Inc/Alamy Stock Photo
38: BorneoRimbawan/Shutterstock
40: Lidia/Shutterstock
45: Raggedstone/Shutterstock
48: Cheryl Senter/MCT/Newscom
51: Warner Bros./Photofest
52: Zeferli/Shutterstock

LIBRARY OF CONGRESS CATALOGING-IN-PUBLICATION DATA

Names: Mooney, Carla, author
Ghost Hunters/by Carla Mooney
Series: Guide to Ghosts and Hauntings
Description: San Diego, CA : ReferencePoint Press, Inc., 2025. |
Includes bibliographical references and index.
 Identifiers: LCCN 2024043946 (print) | ISBN 9781678209940
  (library binding) | ISBN 9781678209957 (ebook)

Spirits and the Spirit World: What People Believe — 4

Introduction — 5
Searching for Spirits

Chapter One — 9
The World of Ghost Hunting

Chapter Two — 19
Ghost-Hunting Teams and Tools

Chapter Three — 29
A Night in the Field

Chapter Four — 37
Ghost Hunting: Science or Pseudoscience?

Chapter Five — 47
Ghost Hunting Meets Pop Culture

Source Notes — 57
For Further Research — 60
Index — 62

SPIRITS AND THE SPIRIT WORLD: WHAT PEOPLE BELIEVE

Belief in Spirits

% of US adults who say . . .

They believe people have a soul or spirit in addition to their physical body	83%
There is something spiritual beyond the natural world, even if we cannot see it	81%
There are some things that science cannot possibly explain	74%
They have had a sudden feeling of connection with something from beyond this world	45%
They have a strong feeling that someone who has passed away was communicating with them from beyond this world	38%
They believe spirits or unseen spiritual forces exist and they have personally encountered one	30%

Communication Between the Living and the Dead

% of US adults who believe it is definitely or probably true that people who have died can . . .

Be united with other loved ones who have already died	57%
Provide assistance, protection, or guidance to the living	46%
Be aware of things going on among the living	44%
Communicate with the living	42%
Be reincarnated	27%
Harm the living	18%

Hearing from the World Beyond

% of US adults who say they . . .

Have had a sudden feeling of connection with someone from beyond this world	45%
Have had a strong feeling that someone who has passed away was communicating with them from beyond this world	38%
Believe spirits or unseen spiritual forces exist and they have personally encountered one	30%

INTRODUCTION

Searching for Spirits

Amy Bruni was eight years old when she saw her first ghost. At the time, Bruni lived with her family in a two-story home in California. One day, while upstairs, Bruni spotted something that looked like a man outside a second-floor window. She was confused about how the man could be so high in the air, and she asked her mother about it. Bruni's mother believed that her daughter had seen something, and she told Bruni that she thought it was a spirit. "I was not afraid; I was intensely curious,"[1] says Bruni.

The ghostly encounter sparked Bruni's life-long fascination with ghosts and paranormal activity. At first, ghost hunting was a hobby, something Bruni did when not at her real job as a project manager for a health insurance company. Outside of work, Bruni researched burial grounds or potential haunted houses. However, when she met the creators of *Ghost Hunters*, a popular television show about ghost hunting, Bruni quit her day job and started ghost hunting full time.

Since then, Bruni has visited hundreds of haunted places worldwide with her ghost-hunting equipment. She has experienced paranormal activity, from seeing spirits to hearing ghostly voices. Bruni has appeared on the ghost-hunting television shows *Kindred Spirits* and *Ghost Hunters* and has also written a book about her ghost-hunting experiences. One of Bruni's favorite parts of ghost hunting is researching the history of places, such as a home or landmark, where people have reported seeing ghosts.

Ghost Hunters, *a popular television show about ghost hunting, has inspired many people to investigate what they believe to be paranormal activity.*

Bruni admits that some people are skeptical about the existence of ghosts and do not believe in her work. Therefore, she insists that exposing false claims about alleged ghost sightings is as important as finding evidence that ghosts exist. She asks skeptics to think about the possibility they might be wrong. She says:

> Trust me, I get it. I can go through life and have some slight experiences and say it's nothing, but I'd rather pay attention to those moments—because what if they're real? What if there's someone there? I'd rather be talking in the dark and be wrong about all of this than ignore it completely. I always tell people that they don't have to be a full-on believer, but just think about if it were you on the other side trying to desperately communicate.[2]

Many Believers

Bruni is not alone in her belief in ghosts and desire to find definitive proof of their existence. Most Americans agree with her. In a 2024 survey, 61.4 percent of respondents said they believed in ghosts, according to RealClear Opinion Research. And 30 percent of American adults report that they have personally encountered a spirit or other unseen spiritual force, according to a separate 2023 Pew Research Center survey.

> "I can go through life and have some slight experiences and say it's nothing, but I'd rather pay attention to those moments—because what if they're real?"[2]
>
> —Amy Bruni, paranormal investigator

One believer is Linda, a nurse who says that she encountered several ghosts when visiting a friend who was seriously ill in the hospital. While reading a book at her friend's bedside, Linda noticed the bed begin to tilt from side to side. "I looked up and saw ten to twelve people standing across the room," she says. "They were dressed in loose clothing. A man sat in a chair, and a child stood next to him. They were talking to one another but made no sound. They looked as if an old antique filter was over them, no color. I look down and up again. They were still there. I figured they were her family waiting for her to cross." After a few minutes, the figures faded away. "My friend survived that night. I have never seen or felt anything like that before,"[3] says Linda.

Curiosity, Not Fear

Stories of ghostly encounters, both believable and questionable, have fueled many people's strong desire to investigate the paranormal and learn more. The introduction of ghost-hunting television shows and other media has brought the work of ghost hunters and their investigations to audiences worldwide. The emergence of the internet as a new place for ghost-hunting enthusiasts and professionals to meet and discuss the latest investigations has further sparked interest in the paranormal and ghost hunting.

As a result, amateur and professional ghost hunters have sprung up across the country and around the world. They search for spirits and investigate reported spirit sightings or paranormal activity. Ghost hunters attempt to find explanations for strange phenomena and find proof of the paranormal. Some work in front of cameras, while others conduct investigations behind the scenes. Both use various tools and techniques in their attempts to capture evidence of a ghostly presence.

Tony Szabelski is a professional paranormal investigator from Chicago, Illinois. He has visited many allegedly haunted locations across the Midwest and has experienced phenomena that he cannot explain, including seeing shadow figures across a room or following a figure down a hallway only to see it disappear. While the thought of being around ghosts may be unsettling for some, Szabelski enjoys it. "Most of the people I know aren't terrified by it. We're curious, maybe even excited by it. The investigation experience varies place by place. You can never really expect anything to happen. You have to go in with an open mind to see what's going to happen,"[4] he says.

CHAPTER ONE

The World of Ghost Hunting

The fascination with the paranormal and the desire to communicate with the dead are as old as human history. Every major ancient civilization, from China to Egypt to Greece, believed in the afterlife and the idea of the soul living on after the body's death. In most of these beliefs, the soul moved on to the world of the dead, but some circumstances could cause the soul to remain or return to the land of the living. Reasons for a soul's return included the need to resolve unfinished business, a violent death, or incomplete or improper burial rites. A death under those circumstances could lead to a soul being caught between the worlds of the living and the dead, unable to move on to the afterlife.

Although many believed in the existence of ghosts, actively trying to talk to ghosts was often frowned on, particularly in Judeo-Christian communities. The Bible's Old Testament instructs believers not to communicate with the dead because it is abhorrent to God. Those who were accused of talking to ghosts of the dead faced punishment. For example, in Great Britain the Act Against Conjuration, Witchcraft, and Dealing with Evil and Wicked Spirits, passed in 1603, provided that invoking or consulting with evil spirits was a felony punishable by death.

Embracing Spiritualism

In the 1800s, views on communicating with the dead began to change in the West. The nineteenth century was a period of rapid innovation and industrialization in the United States and Europe, with many scientific and technological advances. It was also the era of rationalism, in which thinkers held that perception was not the only way to understand the world. Maintaining that reality is logical and intelligible, rationalists insisted that the intellect—through investigation and insight—could comprehend the laws by which the natural world functioned. Guided by this curiosity, the faithful began to look for evidence for their spiritual beliefs, including the existence of ghosts.

Spiritualism, a movement centered on the belief that the living could communicate with the dead through a medium, rose in popularity at this time. In 1848 two sisters from Hydesville, New York, claimed to be able to talk to the dead. Fourteen-year-old Maggie Fox and her eleven-year-old sister, Kate, held a séance and claimed to contact the spirit of a man who was murdered

In the mid-1800s, the Fox sisters traveled across the country with their older sister, holding séances and inviting audiences to hear the rapping noises that proved spirits could communicate from beyond.

in their house several years earlier. The ghost made its presence known and responded to questions by rapping on the walls of the home. The news quickly spread through their community, and the sisters showed off their skills to neighbors in the local town hall. Before

> "There have always been questions about life after death, but in the 19th century, people found new ways to investigate them, using . . . new, cutting-edge technological tools."[5]
>
> —Elisabeth Berry Drago, director at the Science History Institute

long, the Fox sisters traveled across the country, holding séances and inviting audiences to hear the rapping noises that proved spirits could communicate from beyond.

As more people embraced spiritualism, séances were held in drawing rooms across the country. People gathered to talk to their dead loved ones through a medium. Filled by rationalist faith in invention and gadgetry, they often tried communicating with the dead using Ouija boards and other tools. Elisabeth Berry Drago, a director at the Science History Institute, says:

> There have always been questions about life after death, but in the 19th century, people found new ways to investigate them, using these new, cutting-edge technological tools. And part of it was that some of these new tools felt supernatural in and of themselves. The radio, the telegraph, the phonograph. These allowed us to speak over inconceivable distances, communicate instantly from an ocean away, and even preserve human voices in time, and after death.[5]

Holding Séances

In the United States, interest in spiritualism grew after the Civil War. Many who had lost loved ones in the war turned to séances and other methods to contact dead soldiers. Millions of new believers accepted the idea that it was possible to communicate with ghosts. Even when the Fox sisters admitted they had faked their séances in 1888, the spiritualism movement continued to grow. It also crossed the ocean and became popular in Europe. Believers included people from all backgrounds, from rural farmers to scientists and intellectuals.

According to mediums and believers then and now, spirits transmit their messages in various ways. Some spirits use a series of knocks to spell out words. Others communicate through automatic writing, using the medium's hand to write the spirit's message unconsciously. Some spirits send their message through the mouth of a medium who is in a trancelike state.

Leonora Piper was a famous Boston medium who claimed to be able to channel spirits. Piper would go into a trance and unconsciously write messages from the dead. She performed many sittings for customers, and she was able to produce accurate and detailed information about people she did not know. Her abilities drew the attention of scientists, including William James, an American psychologist and philosopher. James had helped found the American Society for Psychical Research (ASPR) in 1884. In a letter to his cousin, James described the ASPR's mission, saying, "Ghosts, second sight, spiritualism, and all sorts of hobgoblins are going to be 'investigated' by the most high-toned and 'cultured' members of the community."[6]

As people increasingly embraced spiritualism, séances were held in hopes that people would be able to communicate with those who had died.

Harry Houdini: Skeptic and Exposer of Frauds

Harry Houdini (1874–1926) was a famous magician, known worldwide for his jaw-dropping escapes from physical restraints. Houdini was also a prominent skeptic of spiritualism and séances. For years, Houdini publicly investigated and debunked hundreds of fake mediums who tricked grieving customers who were desperate to communicate with their deceased loved ones. "This thing they call Spiritualism, wherein a medium intercommunicates with the dead, is a fraud from start to finish," he said. Before his death, Houdini even testified before Congress in 1926 and supported legislation that would have made it a crime for a person to pretend to be able to speak to the dead. Eventually, the proposed legislation was unsuccessful and was never brought to a vote in Congress. A few months after his congressional testimony, Houdini died from a ruptured appendix on Halloween. Ironically, his widow, Bess, held séances for ten years after his death, hoping to contact her late husband. She never did.

Quoted in Bryan Greene, "For Harry Houdini, Séances and Spiritualism Were Just an Illusion," *Smithsonian*, October 28, 2021. www.smithsonianmag.com.

James attended many séances to investigate the mediums. He became interested in Piper after attending one session in which she told him information about his wife's family that no one else knew. James and the ASPR spent years investigating Piper. But James could not reach a definite conclusion about Piper's psychic abilities. "Ultimately, James concluded that there was something meaningful in the Boston medium's work. Within the fragments of her spirit messages and automatic scribblings, he believed there were authentic communications,"[7] says Drago.

Skeptics and Nonbelievers

Not everyone was a believer in spiritualism. Some people who were skeptical that humans could communicate with dead souls set out to show that mediums were scamming the public. In the 1850s British scientist Michael Faraday set out to prove that table turning, a séance activity in which a spirit moved, tilted, or knocked on a table, was fake. At one séance, Faraday secretly insulated the table so it could not be affected by the electrical or magnetic forces that mediums claimed came from spirits. Then he showed that the table's movement was caused by the living participants sitting around it, even unconsciously.

Other skeptics drew the curtain back on methods some mediums used to manipulate their audiences. For example, conducting a séance in dim light created an environment in which participants were more sensitive to sound. Under these conditions, participants were more receptive to the medium's suggestions, especially if they were grieving the death of a loved one. Although many people continued to believe in spiritualism, a lack of hard proof and too many fraudulent mediums dampened some initial enthusiasm for the movement.

The Original Ghost Hunter: Harry Price

In the 1900s several laboratories opened in the United States, Britain, and Europe to establish controlled scientific conditions for investigating ghosts and the supernatural. In London, psychical investigator Harry Price founded the National Laboratory of Psychical Research in 1926. Price's first experience as a ghost hunter occurred when he was only fifteen years old and spent the night with a friend in a manor house rumored to be haunted. They heard eerie footsteps and tried to photograph the ghost. Although unsuccessful in finding proof, the experience cemented Price's interest in ghost hunting.

As an adult, Price joined the Society for Psychical Research in 1920 and spent hours scrutinizing haunted houses and séances, hoping to separate fact from fraud. In one of his investigations, Price debunked the work of spirit photographer William Hope, who claimed to photograph people with their deceased relatives hovering in the frame. Price discovered that Hope was using pre-exposed plates in the camera to create the ghostly effect in his photos.

Price also investigated mediums and tested their psychic abilities. He brought thermometers and other devices to séances to conduct scientific studies. He was able to record some unexplained temperature drops and other phenomena, which convinced him that paranormal activity was real. Price then began

Sir Arthur Conan Doyle's Support for Spiritualism

Sir Arthur Conan Doyle (1859–1930) was a British writer and physician, best known for creating the fictional detective Sherlock Holmes. Conan Doyle was also an outspoken supporter of spiritualism. In 1883 Conan Doyle joined the Society for Psychical Research, along with other scientists, philosophers, and politicians. For many years, Conan Doyle considered himself a novice and experimented with different methods of contacting spirits, such as table turning and automatic writing. He became an enthusiastic supporter of spiritualism after hearing the testimony of several people close to him. When World War I arrived, nearly every family in Britain experienced the loss of a loved one. Conan Doyle believed that he needed to share the message of spiritualism with the world to provide comfort after so many devastating losses. He devoted the rest of his life to spreading spiritualism through public speaking and written works such as *The Land of Mists* (1926) and *The History of Spiritualism* (1926). Until his death in 1930, Conan Doyle traveled worldwide speaking about spiritualism, séances, mediums, and communicating with the dead.

spending more time documenting the paranormal instead of debunking fake mediums.

Price's most famous investigation occurred at the Borley Rectory in Essex, England. Built in 1862, the rectory was rumored to be haunted, with multiple reports of ghost sightings, unexplained noises, and other strange happenings. In 1929 the local newspaper invited Price to investigate the rectory. For several years, Price conducted a careful investigation. He gathered accounts from dozens of witnesses, talking to previous tenants, neighbors, and local townspeople. Price also reported his firsthand accounts, where he claimed to hear and see phenomena such as ringing bells, rapping noises, and objects inexplicably moving from one place to another.

Price carefully documented his findings and methods and created a blueprint for conducting a paranormal investigation. While Price claimed some of his findings supported the existence of paranormal activity, skeptics accused him of exaggerating evidence to support his claims. Regardless, Price's detailed accounts of his work at Borley Rectory had a lasting impact on paranormal research and ghost hunting. He wrote two books on the case that fascinated readers and became bestsellers.

Ed and Lorraine Warren

Ed and Lorraine Warren were two of the most recognized ghost hunters in the United States in the mid-1900s. For several decades, they investigated some of the country's most famous allegedly haunted sites and cofounded the New England Society for Psychic Research in 1952, the region's oldest ghost-hunting organization.

One of the Warrens' most famous paranormal investigations occurred in 1976 at a house in Amityville, New York. In 1975 the Lutz family moved into the Amityville house. The previous year, twenty-three-year-old Ronald DeFeo Jr. had shot and killed his parents and four siblings in the house. The home's new occupants found themselves terrorized by unexplained phenomena. Doors slammed in the middle of the night with no explanation. George Lutz reported that an unseen force held him helpless in bed while his children's beds slammed up and down. Another time, a spirit in the house made his wife levitate and appear to be an old woman. The Lutz family fled the house four weeks after moving in, leaving all their belongings behind.

After being called by a news reporter who had covered the Lutz's story, the Warrens traveled to Amityville to investigate what had happened at the house. They assembled a team of reporters, investigators, and parapsychologists. Inside the home, Ed was pushed to the floor after using a religious symbol in the basement. Lorraine reported being overwhelmed by the sense of a demonic presence and the feeling of being physically pushed. She also had visions of the DeFeo family's bodies on the floor. The Warrens' research team also captured what they believed to be the image of a small boy's spirit. The team researched the property's history, discovering that the Shinnecock Indians had once used it to hold the sick and mentally ill until they died. The Warrens believed that the past suffering on the property had left a negative energy that attracted evil spirits. They concluded that a demonic presence haunted the house. When asked in a 2005

Ronald DeFeo Jr. (pictured with sheriff's deputies) shot and killed his parents and four siblings in their house in Amityville, New York in 1974. The home's later occupants claimed they were terrorized by unexplained phenomena.

interview what it was like to go into the Amityville house, Lorraine replied, "Evil. It's the personification of evil."[8] The Warrens' work at Amityville and other locations inspired numerous books, films, and documentaries.

Over the years, the Warrens wrote several books about their paranormal investigations. They gave lectures and interviews about their experiences. Critics have questioned their claims and accused them of exaggerating or faking their investigations. However, the Warrens' investigations continue to fascinate many people.

Modern Ghost Hunters

Early paranormal investigators such as Price and the Warrens paved the way for modern ghost hunters. Today ghost hunters investigate a wide range of paranormal activities, often focusing on phenomena believed to be related to ghosts. Investigations typically involve visiting sites believed to be haunted or centers of paranormal activity. Reports of paranormal activity include ghostly sightings, the appearance of floating circular or spherical orbs, objects moving on their own, unexplained voices or sounds, fluctuations in electromagnetic fields, cold spots, unexplained odors, and psychic disturbances.

Patty Henderson works in finance during the day and is a paranormal investigator at night with Whispering Souls Paranormal Investigations near Pittsburgh, Pennsylvania. She and her team visit haunted locations and attempt to capture paranormal activity. "Most of the time, people are super fascinated when I tell them I do ghost hunting. They step back; 'That's a thing?' They want to know more. There's more people that are inquisitive about the field than turn away from what we do," Henderson says. The experience of searching for and encountering the unexplained drives Henderson and her Whispering Souls team. "It's like a door that kind of connects our worlds. When the doors open, they come into ours or we go into theirs. That's kind of how we visually see the spirit world. I don't believe that I have a gift. I'm not a psychic, I'm not an empath. I just keep an open mind to strange things that happen,"[9] she says.

> "Most of the time, people are super fascinated when I tell them I do ghost hunting. They step back; 'That's a thing?' They want to know more."[9]
>
> —Patty Henderson, paranormal investigator

Ghost-Hunting Teams and Tools

For Theresa Chick of Somersworth, New Hampshire, the strange activity in her home was deeply unsettling. She heard unexplained sounds, had a toy thrown at her feet by an unknown force, and even saw a ghostly figure in her hallway. Chick installed cameras inside her house to capture video of the activity. She also called the Paranormal Investigators of New England (PI-NE) for help.

PI-NE was formed in 2004 by paranormal investigator Jeffrey Stewart, a private investigator who became interested in ghost hunting after one of his cases involved paranormal activity. He contacted an established Massachusetts ghost-hunting organization in 2001 and trained with its members. A few years later, Stewart launched PI-NE.

Today PI-NE is a team of paranormal investigators based in Vermont who investigate reports of ghosts, spirits, apparitions, and other paranormal activity. "Typically, by the time people reach out to us, they are at a desperation level where they want us there as soon as possible to determine what is happening," says Betty Miller, PI-NE's director. "Most commonly, we hear the client say, 'I just want to know if I'm crazy,' or 'Is this really happening?'"[10]

As a teen, Miller lived in a haunted apartment, which prompted her interest in ghosts and the paranormal. Ghost hunters like Miller and PI-NE rarely investigate paranormal activity alone. Instead, they head out to a case in teams of two or more people.

The team examining camera footage taken by Theresa Chick believed she had captured the image of a spirit. Despite this validation, the ghostly events continue in Chick's home. However, she believes that humans and spirits can amicably coexist, and she has embraced the experience by joining the PI-NE team as an investigator.

Investigating Teams

On a ghost-hunting team, roles can vary depending on the team's size and focus. On smaller teams, members may perform multiple roles during a paranormal investigation, depending on their skills and experience. The team leader, also known as the principal investigator, coordinates the investigation and often has significant experience in paranormal research.

At the beginning of an investigation, researchers often gather background information on a location's history and details about any paranormal activity or hauntings reported. They examine historical records, newspaper articles, and other sources. Interviewers contact witnesses who have experienced paranormal activity at the location and document their firsthand accounts.

In the field, investigators actively participate in investigations, handling and maintaining equipment, observing phenomena, and collecting data. The technicians in the group set up instruments in the field and often operate it. A documentation specialist will take detailed notes throughout the investigation and document observations, conditions, and anything significant.

> "I can go into a space and say, you know, something isn't right or something doesn't feel right."[11]
>
> —Lindsay Stevens, paranormal investigator

Some teams include mediums, or people with psychic abilities. They join investigators in the field to see what insights or impressions they receive. Lindsay Stevens, an investigator with PI-NE, describes herself as very sensitive to paranormal activity. "I can go into a space and say, you know, something isn't right or something doesn't feel right,"[11] she says. Her ability to sense paranormal activity helps her focus the

Paranormal investigators are called in when a resident reports possible paranormal phenomena such as an apparition appearing inside their home.

team on where they should set up equipment. For example, during one investigation, Stevens felt something behind her, touching her hair. Yet nothing was visible to anyone in the room. However, when a team member set up a camera to detect and map entities, it revealed an entity behind her.

After fieldwork, the team's analysts review the data and evidence collected during an investigation. They listen to audio recordings, study photographs and videos, and chart electromagnetic pulse readings. The team will then discuss data and evidence and prepare their findings for their clients. Throughout each stage of a paranormal investigation, effective teamwork and communication are essential for success.

Dowsing Rods

Everything on earth releases energy in some form. Dowsing rods have been used for centuries to detect energy released by objects. For example, some people believe they can locate underground water sources by holding two prongs of a Y-shaped dowsing stick as they pace through an area. When the stick's tip points down, it is supposedly sensing the vibrations that indicate water lies below. Today dowsers still employ the practice to find buried wells or even valuable ores and oil.

Dowsing rods used in paranormal investigations work similarly. Investigators hold two metal L-shaped dowsing rods straight out before them as they try to sense an energy field. While the investigators move around, the rods may cross and form an X to indicate a strong energy. The investigators can then use the rods to ask the spirit yes–no questions in this place. The rods react by crossing or swinging apart as the spirit responds to the questions.

Energy Detectors

Ghost hunters use various devices and equipment to gather evidence of paranormal activity and detect the presence of spirits or ghosts. Most ghost-hunting equipment is designed with the idea that ghosts leave traces in an environment that register as fluctuations in electromagnetic fields. Electromagnetic fields are common and are generated by the movement of electric charges. "In the context of ghost hunting, it is hypothesized that spirits might disrupt or manipulate these fields when they are present. This can be detected and recorded using specialized equipment," says Marina Antoniou, an electrical engineer from the University of Warwick in England. The electromagnetic field meter measures such disruptions. "These detectors are designed to measure the strength and frequency of electromagnetic fields, which can then be analyzed for anomalies. A sudden high spike could relate to something paranormal or just wiring!"[12] says Antoniou.

In addition to electromagnetic recordings, sudden drops in air temperature are believed to occur when a ghost or other paranormal entity is present. To detect temperature changes, ghost-hunting teams often use an infrared thermometer to measure and detect cold spots. When they find fluctuating temperatures, it may indicate areas of potential ghost activity.

Sound and Vision Gear

Most ghost-hunting teams carry a basic digital audio recorder during investigations. Digital audio recorders capture sounds the human ear cannot hear and document electronic voice phenomena (EVP). For Miller, the audio recorder is her most used tool. "There is a never-ending production of new equipment available in the field, and we have a lot, which is fantastic, but it always drives back to the audio recorder," she says. In the field, investigators will make an audio recording of themselves asking questions. Afterward, they will carefully review the recordings and listen for answers hidden in the recording's static. "When you have a voice responding to you through the audio recorder that you did not hear in real-time, you now have something solid that can't be disputed. And that's very exciting,"[13] says Miller.

In the early stages of an investigation, researchers often gather information about a location's history as well as details about any reported paranormal activity.

Closing a Portal

Jen Brujitske is a ghost hunter from Grosse Pointe Woods, Michigan. During each investigation, she uses equipment to scan a location for portals, which she explains are places where spirits can travel back and forth between the worlds of the living and the dead. "They enter and leave from there and visit," she says. Through these portals, Brujitske and her team attempt to communicate with spirits and encourage them to leave. Brujitske's team also uses a device called a hokey pokey box that holds sage and wooden sticks from a palo santo tree. These are burned to release an aroma believed to cleanse a home of spirits after an investigation. "We cleanse the homes to move everything out. We close the portal by telling the spirits to leave and put railroad ties around the perimeter of the home [as a ward against future hauntings]," she says.

Quoted in Meg Leonard, "Spirit Moves Ghost Hunter to Unearth Paranormal Stories," *Grosse Pointe (MI) News*, October 19, 2022. www.grossepointenews.com.

Night vision cameras give investigators eyes in the dark. With these cameras, investigators can see and record phenomena in darkness and low-light conditions. In 2017 ghost hunters from the paranormal team Soul Reapers claimed they captured a child's spirit walking in the hallways of Wentworth Woodhouse, an abandoned manor house in Yorkshire, England. The paranormal investigators visited the location after reports of hauntings at the manor house. They set up night vision cameras, motion sensors, and audio recorders to capture evidence of ghosts. When reviewing their recordings, the team heard a deep growling on one camera when a team member entered the room. Upon closer inspection of their video recordings, the team spotted what they believed to be the ghostly figure of a child.

Some investigators also use a spirit box to capture communications from the dead. A spirit box is like a radio for the paranormal. It quickly scans through radio frequencies, producing a lot of static, or white noise. It is believed that ghosts can use that white noise to communicate with the living through noises, words, or other sounds. Some spirit boxes will record the audio so investigators can listen to it later and play it back more slowly or backward to identify sounds not heard initially. "Everyone has a different frequency and (spirits) answer through the various ones. Sometimes, it's a yes or no answer. At other times, it's a full sentence,"[14] says Jen Brujitske, a ghost hunter from Grosse Pointe Woods, Michigan.

MacKenzie Koncher is a thirty-five-year-old paranormal investigator in Denver, Colorado. She brings several devices to each investigation. She says:

> I bring all kinds of equipment with me when I'm investigating. I bring a spirit box, which is an AM/FM radio transmitter that I believe can allow spirits to communicate. Another co-investigator brings a flashlight, and we ask the spirits to communicate through turning the light on or off to indicate a yes or no answer. We also bring dowsing rods, which are a great way to feel the energy of a room. You can ask the spirit to move the rods (like crossing them to indicate "yes" and straightening them to indicate "no"), and that's a great tool.[15]

Becoming a Ghost Hunter

Equipped with the right tools, ghost hunters are detectives in the world of paranormal activity. They collect evidence, conduct research, and attempt to discover the causes of unexplained phenomena. The path to becoming a ghost hunter is different for everyone. While no formal requirements or degrees are required for paranormal investigators, knowledge about the paranormal and investigative techniques is essential. Some people choose to take online courses in paranormal studies and investigation. For college students, history, psychology, and physical sciences classes can be helpful. Certifications are also available. Reading books, watching documentaries, and attending lectures are ways to learn more about hauntings, paranormal phenomena, and investigation techniques.

> "I bring all kinds of equipment with me when I'm investigating."[15]
>
> —MacKenzie Koncher, paranormal investigator

Many ghost hunting teams carry a small digital audio recorder (pictured) during investigations. Digital audio recorders capture sounds the human ear cannot hear and document Electronic Voice Phenomena (EVPs).

John Kruth is the executive director of the Rhine Research Center in Durham, North Carolina, which offers parapsychology courses and certificates online. He suggests those interested in becoming ghost hunters learn about human biology, physics, and engineering to understand the natural explanations for unexplained phenomena they might encounter during an investigation. "To prepare, you need to learn about the physical world and how it works. If people are under high-powered electrical lines, that can cause electronic problems in the house, affect a person's physical behavior, or cause them to see waves in the air that aren't there,"[16] he says. With this knowledge, investigators can rule out natural explanations before they conclude that paranormal activity is present.

Many people interested in ghost hunting learn from more experienced investigators when getting started. Many ghost-hunting groups will bring new members on investigations so they can learn investigative techniques and how to operate equipment on the job. Paranormal investigator Katrina Weidman says she learned from more experienced ghost hunters. As a child, Weidman was fascinated with ghosts and other paranormal activities. She read every book she could find on the paranormal. In college, she joined a paranormal club. "As luck would have it, there was a paranormal club on campus, the world-renowned Paranormal Research Society (PRS). I trained with them and later worked as their case manager, interviewing thousands of eyewitnesses to the unknown,"[17] she says.

Forming a Team

A shared interest in the paranormal often brings investigators of all levels together. When David Bray and Chris O'Connor met in 2015, their mutual interest in the spirit world and firsthand experiences as mediums led them to start a paranormal team. At first, Bray was hesitant since he had never participated in a formal paranormal investigation. "I was very skeptical going in, and he [O'Connor] actually impressed me so much that we decided to form a group,"[18] says Bray.

Formed in 2016, the Eastern Connecticut Paranormal Society (ECPS) aims to uncover the truth about alleged hauntings. "We actually do more along the lines of debunking and disproving paranormal activity,"[19] says Bray. Since its initial days, the ECPS team has grown to include a photographer, audio producer, researchers, and investigators. After O'Connor died in 2023, Bray remained as the team's medium. The all-volunteer team does about fifty investigations each year, meets with potential clients, and responds to calls and emails about potential paranormal activity.

> "We actually do more along the lines of debunking and disproving paranormal activity."[19]
>
> —David Bray, investigator with Eastern Connecticut Paranormal Society

Working Cases

Many of the calls ECPS receives come from people who believe there is paranormal activity in their private homes. In these cases, the ECPS team attempts to debunk the paranormal claims and give the client a natural explanation for the unexplained happenings. For example, a client from Ansonia, Connecticut, called the team and reported that her four-year-old son was being woken up at night by a ghost. She claimed that she and her son had seen a shadowy figure in the house that spoke to them and made terrifying sounds through a baby monitor.

The team began their investigation by interviewing the family and inspecting the house. They found no evidence of paranormal activity. They pointed out to the mother that a large mirror reflected light from outside streetlamps, causing shadows in the hallway and frightening her son. They also examined the family's baby monitors and discovered that interference from police car radios from a nearby police station caused the unexplained noises heard through the monitors. The team concluded that no paranormal activity existed.

However, in another case, the team reached a different conclusion. After Pamela Lamson's seven-year-old daughter, Heather, died from cancer, Lamson felt that her daughter's spirit still lingered at their home. Years later, after meeting Bray and O'Connor, Lamson's son and daughter-in-law invited the ECPS team to their home. While there, O'Connor discovered that Heather's spirit was present. The team used a spirit box to make contact. "First, I was afraid. I couldn't believe what I was hearing. Then, when he asked her what her favorite color was and she said purple, you could hear it really well. It was her. It makes me happy to know she's around,"[20] says Lawson.

Cases like these demonstrate that clients turn to investigators because they want explanations for unusual experiences. Paranormal team members act professionally and sympathetically to comfort clients and assure them that their concerns are valid. Whether a streetlight's shadow or a voice from beyond, the conclusions that ghost hunters draw help clients find resolution to mysteries that haunt them.

CHAPTER THREE

A Night in the Field

After John and Renee Von Klopp moved their business, Razor Sharp Screen Printing, to a new building in Sun Prairie, Wisconsin, they quickly realized something was unusual about the new location. "We were having noises, smells, and just very subtle little things that just raise the hairs on the back on your neck,"[21] says Renee. The couple and their daughter heard footsteps walking across the upper floors when no one was there. A toy train turned on and off without human help. And their dog, Duke, started growling at empty corners in the building. "We didn't have chairs flying across the room or anything like that,"[22] says Renee. But there were enough unexplained occurrences that the Von Klopps called for professional help. They turned to Paranormal of Wisconsin, a team of paranormal investigators based in Dane County, Wisconsin.

Preliminary Work and Research

When a call comes in about potential ghostly activity, much work must be done before paranormal investigators head out into the field. Jason Bertram, a former police officer, is a lead investigator and cofounder of Paranormal of Wisconsin. He recognizes that the people who call his four-person team are reaching out for help. "Our big thing is when they call us, when they reach out to us, they are in need. They are confused, they are scared, there's a lot of things going on,"[23] says Bertram.

> "Usually, people don't know how much research goes into it. I used to get old newspapers through interlibrary loan and look at them through microfilm readers. We're always looking for stories, for history, to back up the ghost stories and sightings."[24]
>
> —Tony Szabelski, paranormal investigator

Bertram's team follows a thorough process to determine whether a house is haunted. First, Bertram asks a new client many questions about what they have experienced and what they know about the site's history. With this information, the team typically resolves about 70 percent of new cases over the phone as not being paranormal occurrences.

If the mystery is not solved during a phone call, the investigators research the history of the building or location. They may research online, search through library sources, and consult with a local historical society or expert. Tony Szabelski, a paranormal investigator from Chicago, often stops at the library to research before investigating at the alleged haunted location. "Usually, people don't know how much research goes into it. I used to get old newspapers through interlibrary loan and look at them through microfilm readers. We're always looking for stories, for history, to back up the ghost stories and sightings,"[24] he says.

When the Paranormal of Wisconsin team researched the Von Klopp's building in Sun Prairie, they discovered that it used to be a funeral parlor in the 1800s. "The fact that it used to be a funeral parlor—so when you have so many emotions tied into a death of a loved one or what have you—it brings a lot of interesting details for an investigation,"[25] says Bertram.

Paranormal investigator Thomas D'Agostino agrees that research is essential to any paranormal investigation. He tries to uncover as much history as possible before going into the field, learning about the site's history and the people involved. "We search through records and try to establish some timeline or era that may be pertinent to the alleged paranormal occurrences,"[26] says D'Agostino. He also researches any current activity and people connected to the site so he can evaluate whether the reported activity is truly paranormal or if there is a more natural explanation for what is happening. He looks for information about "any modifications or restorations currently taking place, name, age, and relation of the people affected and the condition of the mental and physical state of the people involved. There is a lot to be ruled out before knowing what to rule in,"[27] says D'Agostino.

Preparing for a Site Visit

Before fieldwork, the paranormal team will also conduct a site assessment, obtain any required permissions from local authorities or private owners, and set expectations with clients. Over the years, there have been numerous occasions when ghost hunters have entered a reportedly haunted site without permission and have subsequently been arrested and charged with trespassing on private property. In Sugar Land, Texas, for example, an abandoned prison has been a tempting site for ghost hunters. According to Sugar Land police captain Pete Lara, motion-activated security cameras at the prison show multiple people breaking through the property's fences to get inside each week. "We get a lot of folks that are fascinated with ghost hunting," Lara says. However, he warns that trespassing on the property is illegal and dangerous because of broken glass, exposed beams, and holes

Visiting locations such as abandoned prisons can be dangerous, due to broken glass, exposed beams, and holes in the floor. In addition, if investigators enter such sites without permission, they risk being arrested for trespassing.

in the floor. He warns people to stay away, or they will be arrested and charged with criminal trespassing. "We take it serious. We want to make sure we send a message out there that we don't want folks on the property,"[28] says Lara.

Investigators will also prepare any safety precautions needed in the field. One of the most important safety precautions is never going to an investigation site alone. While many people are afraid of ghosts, the reality is that living people are more likely to be a problem. Therefore, investigators should choose clients and cases carefully, as advised by John Kruth, the Rhine Research Center executive director. "When someone calls you to go to their house, you don't know what you're walking into. You have to be cautious and this is where trusting your instincts is important. If it doesn't seem right, don't do it,"[29] says Kruth. To protect everyone, paranormal investigators should work with at least one partner in case something goes wrong on an investigation, either with the client or the site.

> "When someone calls you to go to their house, you don't know what you're walking into. You have to be cautious and this is where trusting your instincts is important. If it doesn't seem right, don't do it."[29]
>
> —John Kruth, Rhine Research Center executive director

In the Field

Once the preliminary work has been completed, the investigative team is ready to head into the field. Many teams will conduct a walk-through of the site to familiarize themselves with its layout and identify any potential hazards, such as areas with poor lighting or unsafe conditions. During a walk-through, investigators will also note any unusual smells, sounds, or feelings they experience.

One night in November 2023, paranormal investigator Eli Freund and members of the ECPS team set up equipment at a house in Winsted, Connecticut. The home's occupants reported seeing ghostly figures on the third floor, including a female wearing a white dress, a child in modern dress with a bowl haircut, and an older man wearing a long-sleeve shirt and dress shoes. The occupants also reported hearing a door open and close loudly in

Investigating for Free

Most paranormal investigators are so passionate about their work, they will take on cases without being paid. For many investigators, the main goal of their work is to help people having trouble with unexplained activity, and many believe that charging a fee for their services is inappropriate in most cases. "[If] you run into a team that charges you, you need to run because they are not out to help you, they're out to make a buck," says Ellen MacNeil, the founder of SPIRITS of New England. Most investigators also hold full-time jobs to fund their investigations. However, there are a few exceptions to the no-payment rule. When invited to speak at a lecture or investigate a public place, many paranormal investigators will accept payment. Other options include writing books or creating podcasts that generate revenue. Some ghost hunters even take on side work as tour guides at well-known haunted sites.

Quoted in Shayna Murphy, "11 Secrets of Paranormal Investigators," Mental Floss, October 14, 2022. www.mentalfloss.com.

the middle of the night, hearing footsteps, and seeing dark shadows. At the home, the six-person investigative team split into two groups: three in the attic and three in the basement. They set up electronic recording equipment in each location.

Once the team was satisfied, the video cameras began recording, and investigators attempted to contact any spirits in the home. "Can you tell us your name?" an investigator asks on the video. "Let us know you're here." There are a few seconds of silence as the investigators wait for a response. Then, more questions. "Did you die here?" and "Why are you here?"[30] There were no answers. They placed a box near the stairs. The box's glowing red light was supposed to change color if a spirit came near. However, it remained red.

Next, investigators brought out a new device, a spirit box, to detect whether there were any spirits nearby. "A spirit box is this handheld device that sweeps through radio waves . . . super, super quickly. Sometimes what happens is we get little blips of radio that seep through, you know, you hear a little bit of music or hear a fraction of a word,"[31] says Freund. This time, the spirit box released short bursts of white noise and nothing else. There were

Residual vs. Intelligent Hauntings

Not all hauntings are the same. Residual hauntings occur when a ghost is seen repeatedly doing the same thing over and over and are the most common type of haunting experienced by most people. Paranormal experts believe that residual hauntings happen when energy from emotional events leave an imprint on the living world. The release of this energy creates the ghostly form or scenes. "In these instances, it doesn't usually interact with you. It just kind of goes through the same routine over and over. It's almost like they're stamped in space and time," says Stephanie Pinkey, an investigator with Paranormal Investigators of North Dakota. In contrast, intelligent hauntings occur when a ghost interacts or communicates with living people. The spirit has remained connected to a living person, place, or thing. It may be compelled to deliver a message or watch over living loved ones. This type of haunting often appears as moving objects, doors opening and closing, strange sounds, disturbances of electrical devices, and other efforts to get the attention of the living.

Quoted in *Fargo Monthly*, "Interview with the Experts: A Q&A with the Paranormal Investigators of North Dakota," 2022. https://fargomonthly.com.

no voices, no music, no sounds. The investigators repeatedly attempted to make contact, but nothing changed. "It could just be that there is nothing to get,"[32] says one investigator. Most ECPS cases end this way, with no evidence of paranormal activity. "I'd say 5 to 10 percent of all cases that we go on actually have paranormal activity going on. Even further, we only take about 10 percent of the cases that come into us,"[33] says Freund.

Next, the team investigated the location using equipment including electromagnetic field detectors and recording devices. They attempted to talk to spirits and ask questions. Although they might not hear the spirits' responses in person, voices and other noises sometimes become apparent when the team replays and listens to the investigation recordings later.

Often, Jason Bertram's team spends multiple nights at the same location to create a connection with the spirits there. The team stayed overnight at the Von Klopp's building twice to investigate. They reported being able to communicate with the ghosts in the building and recorded their interactions. The team concluded that the ghosts were most likely the spirits of people whose bodies had been in the funeral parlor. The team assured the Von Klopps that the ghosts did not have any bad intentions toward them. The Von Klopps decided to remain in the building. "The ghosts seem to be very friendly and they seem to be very interested in what's going on. The things they are doing are just things to let us know they are around—to kind of catch our attention,"[34] says Renee Von Klopp.

Reviewing the Findings

After a night in the field, a paranormal team's work continues. They review the collected recordings, photographs, sensor data, and other evidence. Tanya Vandesteeg, a paranormal investigator in Memphis, Tennessee, says:

> We set up cameras, motion detectors, and our team will go through all of the footage. A lot of it is putting headphones on and listening to see if there are any voices we didn't pick up while we were there—those are called EVPs, electronic voice phenomena. We compile all the footage, and we come back with the client. We're like, "Okay, this is what we found. This is what we didn't find."[35]

After a night in the field, a paranormal team review the data from sensors as well as photographs and sound recordings.

> "If you're a paranormal investigator, you've gotta go through all your tape recorders, all your cameras, and everything, and it takes hours to do that, and you may not find anything, and then you might find just half a second of something that you cannot explain."[36]
>
> —Ellen MacNeil, founder of SPIRITS of New England

Ellen MacNeil, the founder of SPIRITS of New England, has been investigating ghosts, hauntings, and other paranormal activities with her team since 2009. She says that real-life investigations are incredibly time consuming and often involve hours of work that result in only a few seconds of evidence. "If you're a paranormal investigator, you've gotta go through all your tape recorders, all your cameras, and everything, and it takes hours to do that, and you may not find anything, and then you might find just half a second of something that you cannot explain,"[36] she says.

Not like on TV

Paranormal investigator Anthony Duda cautions clients and others interested in ghost hunting that most investigations are nothing like what is shown on ghost-hunting reality television shows. In real life, the investigations are often much slower paced and often provide little evidence. Duda says:

> Most of the time, nothing happens. . . . [It's] not like a circus, [these ghosts] don't perform on command. That's why ghost-hunting groups that see a lot of this stuff on TV [have] such high turnover, because people get bored so quickly. They think it's like what it's like on TV, and [forget] that these shows are edited. And they sit around for hours on these investigations, and they get disillusioned, bored, and off they go, because it's not like that.[37]

Dedicated ghost hunters have patience. They believe in their work and are curious to learn more about things that have no easy explanation. They also enjoy helping clients find answers to and make peace with their paranormal experiences.

CHAPTER FOUR

Ghost Hunting: Science or Pseudoscience?

For many years, scientists have attempted to prove the existence of ghosts and investigate paranormal phenomena. Paranormal investigators set up in abandoned buildings, historic homes, and cemeteries to gather data and evidence of the ghostly energy that they believe exists. However, none have been able to reproduce their results in a controlled experiment under controlled conditions. Until they can do so, skeptics argue that ghost hunting must remain firmly in the realm of pseudoscience.

Scientific Work

Even most serious paranormal investigators rely heavily on skepticism during their investigations. They first attempt to disprove any paranormal activity reports by finding natural explanations for unusual phenomena. "(They're) attempting to essentially separate the wheat from the chaff until you're left with things that you can't explain through natural means,"[38] says Marc Eaton, head of Ripon College's sociology and anthropology departments in Ripon, Wisconsin.

In looking at experiences or events that cannot be easily explained, paranormal investigators insist that their work is a legitimate science. *Encyclopaedia Britannica* defines *science* as "any system of knowledge that is concerned with the physical world

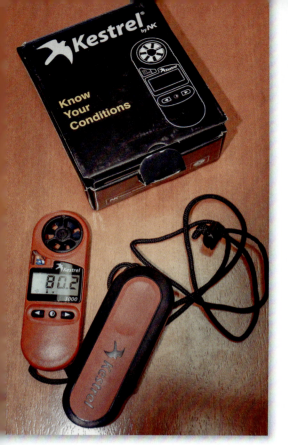

Some paranormal investigators use instruments such as Kestrel meters (pictured), which continuously track air movement, temperature, barometric pressure, and more.

and its phenomena and that entails unbiased observations and systematic experimentation."[39] Under this definition, many paranormal investigators see their work as pioneering science. "They're confident that with the latest technologies and what might be coming down the road in five, 10 (and) 15 years, that they might be able to finally be the people who definitively prove that there's some form of life or some form of consciousness that exists beyond death,"[40] Eaton says.

Eaton interviewed numerous investigators as part of his research into paranormal investigations. Many investigators rely on a technology- and science-based approach to their work. They use technological tools to monitor, measure, and gather data during an investigation. Their expensive, high-tech equipment includes night-vision cameras, electromagnetic frequency readers, motion detectors, barometric pressure sensors, and vibration detectors.

Paranormal investigators use tools initially designed for other scientific purposes. For example, Kestrel meters were originally designed to measure wind speed, temperature, and other weather conditions and calculate wind chill and dew point metrics. In paranormal investigations, Kestrel meters are set up to continuously track air movement, temperature, barometric pressure, and more. Paranormal investigators believe that unexplained temperature changes can be a sign of ghosts or other paranormal activity. The meters provide accurate and objective temperature data, allowing investigators to identify any significant changes that might occur where paranormal activity is reported. These and other tools help investigators examine unusual happenings and often find natural explanations for them.

Researching the Paranormal

Recognizing that science and technology are key to understanding the uncommon and the unknown, numerous colleges and universities offer opportunities for scientists and students to research and study parapsychology and paranormal phenomena. Parapsychology is the study of psychic phenomena such as near-death experiences, telepathy, and clairvoyance. At the University of Virginia, researchers with the Division of Perceptual Studies (DOPS) study evidence for the survival of consciousness after death, out-of-body experiences, and other psychic phenomena. DOPS is part of the university's Department of Psychiatry and Neurobehavioral Sciences.

Parapsychology

Parapsychology is the scientific study of several psychic phenomena and the search for proof of their existence. The field began in the 1930s when its founder, Joseph Banks Rhine, and his colleagues at Duke University began to study extrasensory perception. Today parapsychologists study psychic phenomena that include precognition, clairvoyance, telepathy, extrasensory perception, telekinesis, and out-of-body experiences. Precognition is the ability to see the future in a vision or dream. Clairvoyance is the ability to see information from a distant location, while telepathy is the ability for two people to communicate through their minds without the use of speech or other senses. Extrasensory perception is the ability to sense things beyond the usual five senses, and telekinesis is the ability to move objects with the mind. In out-of-body experiences, people see their physical body as if they were floating above it. Parapsychology also includes the study of ghosts and hauntings. The general term *psi* (pronounced like "sigh") is used for the psychic phenomena studied in parapsychology.

Reports of near-death experiences by patients have caused some physicians to believe that people can leave their physical bodies behind and experience things that go beyond the mortal plane. These experiences happen when people are unconscious or have been pronounced dead.

Bruce Greyson, a professor of psychiatry and neurobehavioral sciences, researches near-death experiences at DOPS. "I was raised in a scientific household, where things that couldn't be seen, heard, or felt were never discussed. Our world was the physical world, and the idea that there was anything else never came up. When you died, that was the end,"[41] says Greyson. Shortly after Greyson finished medical school, however, a patient's near-death experience sparked his interest in the phenomenon. He decided the best way to understand these experiences and find logical explanations was to research them in depth. Greyson says:

> Over the past five decades, I've interviewed thousands of people who were brought back from the threshold of death—or in some cases pronounced dead—and had striking tales to tell. Although it's impossible to say for certain what happens when we die, I have heard hundreds of accounts of people claiming to have left their

physical bodies and seeing things they shouldn't have been able to see while they were unconscious. . . . This has affected me in subtle but definite ways. I no longer believe that the physical world is all there is, or even that it is the most important part of our world. I don't know whether we survive bodily death, but I take the possibility seriously. I feel comfortable with the unknown and not having to have all the answers.[42]

In Scotland the University of Edinburgh's Koestler Parapsychology Unit is a small research group within the school's psychology department. Caroline Watt leads the unit's research in parapsychology and the paranormal. She strives to follow rigorous scientific protocols when testing psychic phenomena. Watt says:

So long as you conduct the research well, so it's well-controlled research, then it's accepted at least amongst my colleagues here at Edinburgh. And some of this work is published in mainstream psychology journals, as well, so it has a foothold in mainstream psychology, but you really have to work hard to demonstrate that you're doing proper science—it's not a pseudoscience: You're testing hypotheses, you're thinking about possible flaws in the design and trying to rule them out. So a lot of our time in parapsychology is spent trying to show other researchers that we know what we're doing as scientists.[43]

Drawing in Respected Scientists

Some respected scientists have ventured into ghost hunting and paranormal investigation. Noah Leigh is a career scientist with an undergraduate degree in biology and graduate degrees in epidemiology and cell biology. In 2007 Leigh started a paranormal investigation team, Paranormal Investigators of Milwaukee (PIM). With PIM, Leigh uses his scientific training during

> "We have a 'debunk-first' mentality, and that's reflected in our cases."[44]
>
> —Noah Leigh, scientist who investigates paranormal activity

each paranormal investigation. "We have a 'debunk-first' mentality, and that's reflected in our cases,"[44] he says. Leigh admits that most of his work involves disproving the paranormal. He says:

It's really satisfying when we can replicate a photograph [of an alleged ghost] or an experience and demonstrate how something that seemed paranormal at first really isn't. We see our purpose as educational, providing a public service. When we do an investigation and interview people, there's a lot of genuine fear because they can't explain what's going on, and we're very sensitive to that.[45]

PIM does not use mediums or psychics but prefers cameras, digital audio recorders, and other instruments to collect data during investigations. The team also relies on the scientific method, a process used by scientists in all fields to observe, ask questions, and search for answers using carefully designed tests and experiments. Leigh says:

We do bring more scientific rigor to the process. We make actual reports—a lot of investigators don't—and we document as much as we can. We use equipment, but not the stuff you see on TV. So much of that is ridiculously expensive and useless most of the time. Low-quality equipment is subject to interference and gives you lots of false positives. Plenty of investigators are fine with that, it makes for more drama, but that's not how we operate.[46]

Leigh understands that many in the scientific community dismiss his work as pseudoscience. "If you do it right, the investigations themselves aren't pseudoscientific," he says. "It's the method behind the investigation and the people conducting it. A lot of teams are biased—they already believe in the paranormal, so they will be looking at whatever evidence they gather to support that belief. That's not how we work. We always have a questioning mindset."[47]

The Case for Pseudoscience

While believers argue that ghost hunting is a science, most academics and skeptics consider ghost hunting to be a pseudoscience, a set of practices that are mistakenly thought to be based on science and the scientific method. Skeptics point out that no scientific study has confirmed the existence of ghosts. They contend that investigations have been able to produce little measured, objective data to support the existence of ghosts, and experiment conditions have few controls to ensure reliability of the results. Skeptics also argue that without objective data, paranormal investigators rely too heavily on anecdotal evidence and personal testimonies that can be biased and manipulated.

Researchers often find alternate explanations for paranormal phenomena when scientific rigor is applied to paranormal investigations. In one study, researchers replicated the feeling of an unseen

Committee for Skeptical Inquiry

The Committee for Skeptical Inquiry is an organization with the primary mission of debunking claims of the paranormal. The organization, formerly known as the Committee for the Scientific Investigation of Claims of the Paranormal (CSICOP), was originally founded in 1976 when skeptics were concerned about increasing public interest in the paranormal. At the time, CSICOP executive director Lee Nisbet explained the organization's view that belief in the paranormal was "a very dangerous phenomenon. Dangerous to science, dangerous to the basic fabric of our society. . . . We feel it is the duty of the scientific community to show that these beliefs are utterly screwball." Some of the organization's founding members included scientists, academics, and science writers, including Carl Sagan, Isaac Asimov, and Ray Hyman. Today the organization maintains a network of people interested in critical examination of paranormal and fringe science. It publishes a bimonthly journal, *Skeptical Inquirer*, that examines claims of the paranormal.

Quoted in Skeptical About Skeptics, "The Committee for Skeptical Inquiry." https://skepticalabout skeptics.org.

> "Just as using a calculator doesn't make you a mathematician, using a scientific instrument doesn't make you a scientist."[48]
>
> —Benjamin Radford, editor of *Skeptical Inquirer* magazine

presence by tricking participants' brains into misperceiving the body's signals. Other studies have linked visions of ghosts or spirits with experiencing sleep paralysis.

While some scientists approach paranormal investigations with an emphasis on the scientific method and gathering objective, measurable data, many others do not. Many ghost hunters use more subjective methods, such as mediums and psychics, to locate and identify ghosts and other paranormal activity.

Even the use of high-tech equipment in paranormal investigations can be problematic. If an inexperienced person does not use equipment properly, the device's data is unreliable. "Just as using a calculator doesn't make you a mathematician, using a scientific instrument doesn't make you a scientist,"[48] says Benjamin Radford, editor of *Skeptical Inquirer* magazine.

Additionally, skeptics point out that no proof exists that any of the instruments and devices used in paranormal investigations work like ghost hunters say they do. Radford explains:

> The uncomfortable reality that ghost hunters carefully avoid—the elephant in the tiny, haunted room—is, of course, that no one has ever shown that any of this equipment actually detects ghosts. The supposed links between ghosts and electromagnetic fields, low temperatures, radiation, odd photographic images, and so on are based on nothing more than guesses, unproven theories, and wild conjecture. If a device could reliably determine the presence or absence of ghosts, then by definition, ghosts would be proven to exist.[49]

Alternate Explanations

Many times, unexplained sounds, sights, and other alleged paranormal phenomena are revealed to result from a natural cause. Kenny Biddle is a paranormal skeptic and science enthusiast. He approaches each case as if it is a puzzle to be solved. "I do my best to solve a mystery. My goal is to gather enough information that will lead to a solid and honest conclusion that sufficiently explains a mystery. I want to be the real-life Scooby-Doo gang,"[50] says Biddle.

Biddle once believed in the paranormal, but now he is firmly on the side of skeptics. He became an expert in photography, the interaction of light and film, and digital sensors. He says many photos of "ghostly figures" have a more earthly explanation. "I began understanding how popular paranormal images were being captured. They were from operator errors, optical illusions, and a gross misunderstanding of the science of photography,"[51] says Biddle. For example, glowing orbs can be caused by a camera flash reflecting off microscopic dust particles. An ectoplasmic mist is simply the photographer's breath rising in front of a camera lens, while ghostly figures are often the result of long-exposure photography. Biddle also explains that equipment that detects paranormal energy will respond to any electromagnetic field and could be triggered by two-way radios.

Skeptics say that supposedly paranormal phenomena such as glowing orbs can be caused by a camera's flash reflecting off floating dust particles.

In one case, Biddle visited the historic Knickerbocker Hotel in Linesville, Pennsylvania. The hotel is no longer open to the public, but Biddle was invited to the property by owner Peg Knickerbocker, along with several other ghost-hunting teams. The hotel was known for being the site of paranormal activity, including ghostly figures and a haunted doll.

During his visit, Biddle investigated several of the hotel's paranormal occurrences, including the haunted doll. The doll was said to be able to change its facial expression from an everyday face to an angry or evil expression. The hotel had two photographs of the doll that appeared to capture proof of the doll's changing facial expressions.

However, when Biddle examined the doll and the photographs, he made several observations. The two photographs used slightly different positioning and lighting. A flash illuminated the doll's face and eyes in the first photo. However, the flash was not used in the second photo, and the doll appeared to be slightly repositioned. The changes in position and lighting between the two photographs caused the doll's face to appear darker, created shadows and made its glass eyes appear black in one photo. "This was not a case of a doll pulling a 'Chucky' (from the beloved horror movie franchise) but rather selective lighting by someone (not by the hotel's owner) trying to promote the idea it was haunted or possessed,"[52] says Biddle.

The Search for Proof Continues

Those who believe in ghosts and the paranormal insist that just because something cannot be seen does not mean it does not exist. They point to established sciences, including biology, chemistry, and physics, that deal with objects the human eye cannot see. In this viewpoint, the science of ghost hunting will move forward when technology advances enough to capture definitive proof of the existence of ghosts. For many others, however, ghost hunting will remain a pseudoscience as long as the existence of ghosts remains unproven.

Ghost Hunting Meets Pop Culture

Ghost hunting has become a prominent part of pop culture, captivating audiences with its blend of mystery, suspense, and the supernatural. Television shows like *Ghost Hunters* and *Paranormal State* have gained widespread popularity, depicting teams of investigators using high-tech equipment to explore allegedly haunted locations. These programs often feature eerie night-vision footage, EVP, and dramatic encounters with unseen entities, all designed to thrill viewers and fuel fascination with the unknown. Beyond television, ghost hunting has spawned books, podcasts, and even tourist attractions centered on haunted sites worldwide, making it an engaging and enduring aspect of modern popular entertainment.

Reality Television

Ghost hunting on television has emerged as a fascinating blend of entertainment and pseudoscientific investigation. Shows like *Ghost Hunters*, one of the first to explore ghost hunting for a television audience, emphasized sophisticated equipment and scientific methods to explore alleged haunted locations. *Ghost Hunters* and other similar programs often feature teams of investigators that record and document their experiences, from changes in temperature and electromagnetic fluctuations to unexplained audio recordings of sounds made by unseen spirits. These shows hold viewers' attention by including personal narratives in the storylines and highlighting the emotional and physical toll of ghost hunting on the show's stars, the paranormal investigators.

Ghost Hunters is the original ghost-hunting reality television show. In each episode, Jason Hawes, Grant Wilson, and a team of real-life paranormal investigators from the Atlantic Paranormal Society investigate reported paranormal activity in the country's most haunted sites. The original series debuted in 2004 and ran for eleven seasons until 2016. The popular series was revived in 2019 and released its sixteenth season in 2023. *Ghost Hunters* fan Rae Alexandra explains why she watched the show. "My initial interest in *Ghost Hunters*, then, sprang from the idea that folks could gather tangible proof of the paranormal—be it video footage, photos, voice recordings, or light and sound interactions—and treat it like science instead of superstition,"[53] she says.

Jason Hawes (left) and Grant Wilson are the hosts of the popular reality television series, Ghost Hunters. *The show was so popular that it spawned a new genre of shows on television.*

The popularity of *Ghost Hunters* launched numerous spin-offs and related reality shows focused on paranormal investigations, each with its spin on the paranormal. One long-running show, *Ghost Adventures*, first aired in 2008 and continued to produce new episodes in 2024. *Ghost Adventures* follows real-life ghost hunters Zak Bagans, Aaron Goodwin, Billy Tolley, and Jay Wasley as they investigate sites said to be haunted. Over the years, Bagans and his team have captured what they say are disembodied voices, apparitions, and moving objects. They claim to have been touched, pushed, and scratched by invisible entities.

Bagans is undeniably the star of the show. Over the years, he has gathered millions of fans who follow his ghostly adventures. In each investigation, Bagans speaks to spirits and attempts to convince them to come forward and communicate with his team. Bagans claims he is very sensitive to paranormal energy, which can make him feel startled, scared, sad, or overwhelmed. Sometimes, an encounter with paranormal energy can even make him physically ill. He says:

> I'm a magnet for energies, and I can't turn that off. I'm a hyper-empathic person. . . . You start crying, I'm probably going to start crying too. There's someone bad in the room, I'll sense that, and it'll give me a headache. I can't turn it off. Within the human brain and the conscious mind, there is an electromagnetic energy field. When you die, that electromagnetic field doesn't disintegrate. Ghosts have an electrical charge to them, and I'm sensitive to that. I feel it, I'll get those goosebumps. I'll feel that static charge.[54]

Ghost Hunting in the Movies

On the big screen, movies have also featured ghost hunting and paranormal activity, blending horror, suspense, and supernatural activity. Many of these films are inspired by real-life paranormal cases, including *The Amityville Horror* (1979), *Poltergeist* (1982), and *The Conjuring* (2013). *The Amityville Horror* tells the story of the Lutz family and the terrifying supernatural activity they experienced after moving into an old house that was the site of a mass murder. The movie became a horror classic, led to several sequels, and inspired a 2005 remake.

Three years later, in 1982, one of the most iconic horror movies, *Poltergeist*, was produced by legendary director Steven Spielberg. The movie follows the Freeling family moving into a new home and experiencing unexplained, paranormal events. At first, the unusual activity appears harmless, such as objects moving around the house. However, the paranormal activity turns increasingly hostile, and unseen spirits kidnap the youngest daughter. The family turns to a paranormal investigator for help. Although the film is fictional, it was inspired by an alleged haunting in the 1950s involving the Hermann house in Long Island, in which the family brought in a paranormal investigator to examine unexplained activity such as moving objects and popping bottles.

Ghost Hunting in Books

Ghost hunting and paranormal investigations appear in literature across a wide variety of genres. Nonfiction accounts detail the experiences of real-life investigations and paranormal investigators like Amy Bruni and Steve Gonsalves. How-to books offer detailed instructions for becoming a ghost hunter and conducting a paranormal investigation. Novels blend tales of ghost hunters and paranormal activity into stories that entertain readers of all ages.

One classic 1959 novel, *The Haunting of Hill House* by Shirley Jackson, tells the story of four people who meet at the reputedly haunted Hill House and begin to experience strange events, including ghostly visions, unexplained noises, and strange writing appearing on the walls. Since it was first published, the book has become a horror classic. Author Neil Gaiman chose *The Haunting of Hill House* as the scariest book he has ever read. "The books that have profoundly scared me when I read them—made me want to sleep with the light on, made the neck hairs prickle and the goose bumps march, are few," he says. "But Shirley Jackson's *The Haunting of Hill House* beats them all: a maleficent house, real human protagonists, everything half-seen or happening in the dark. It scared me as a teenager and it haunts me still."

Quoted in *New York Times*, "The Book That Terrified Neil Gaiman. And Carmen Maria Machado. And Dan Simmons," July 16, 2018. www.nytimes.com.

This scene from the movie The Conjuring *depicts two ghost hunters investigating reported paranormal activity at an old Rhode Island farmhouse. The original film and its sequels have been very popular in the horror film genre.*

Released in 2013, *The Conjuring* tells the story of Carolyn and Roger Perron as they move their family into an old Rhode Island farmhouse. Unexplained things start happening, and unseen forces begin terrorizing the family. Desperate for answers, the Perrons call paranormal investigators Ed and Lorraine Warren to check it out. The movie is based on one of the Warrens' most famous real-life paranormal investigations and the experiences of the Perron family. The film's success inspired several sequels, making *The Conjuring* franchise one of the most successful horror franchises in box office history.

Entertainment vs. Authenticity

Ghost-hunting reality shows and movies have brought paranormal investigation into pop culture, making celebrities out of camera-ready investigators and sparking a growing interest in ghosts and hauntings nationwide. Ghost-hunting reality shows and movies get

Professional filmmakers say that some paranormal phenomena, such as shadows, light orbs, and shadowy figures, typically have natural explanations or are manipulated to look real.

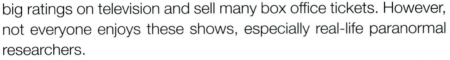

big ratings on television and sell many box office tickets. However, not everyone enjoys these shows, especially real-life paranormal researchers.

Paranormal researchers have always struggled against the perception that they are fakes and hacks. Mainstream science has long viewed paranormal research with suspicion because it lacks objective, measurable evidence. However, some scientists continue searching for evidence that paranormal phenomena exist, and they believe that ghost-hunting reality shows are making their job more difficult. According to Andrew Nichols, a psychologist and parapsychologist, television ghost hunters often push bad science on viewers. He points out that television shows only conduct investigations at night, when the darkness makes good observation difficult. Investigators use unproven instruments that appear to be scientific but are unable to produce reliable results. Investigators are too quick to suggest that every odd sound, orb, or supposed cold spot is a sign of a ghost, even if natural causes can explain them.

Ghost-hunting reality shows have been accused of prioritizing entertainment over authenticity. Even worse, some critics claim that some on-screen events are faked. Many of these shows rely on tricks of the television industry to create a paranormal atmosphere for viewers. Filmmaker Brooks Vernon says:

A large part of it is the performance of those involved. The hosts will jump and say something touched them, or they heard a noise or hit a cold spot. That part is easy to fake, but these shows also rely on the power of suggestion, ambiguous footage, and equally suspicious audio. The human brain always tries to fill in various blanks and see patterns where there aren't necessarily any to be found. This means that in a bid to make things feel more like a paranormal horror movie, investigators on these shows would set up an EVP (electronic voice phenomena) recording and get a bunch of incoherent static as a result, but if the host says within the static is the phrase "help me," and the show plays that static back multiple times in a row with a little "help me" subtitle underneath, a person's brain will do the work to convince themselves that the static really is saying "help me."[55]

Vernon explains that television shows often manipulate video footage to present shadows, light orbs, and shadowy figures. Although these sights typically have natural explanations, ghost-hunting shows will often quickly suggest the paranormal is at work. "If they play the right few seconds of footage any number of times and edit the sequence properly, they could convince just about anyone,"[56] says Vernon.

Mustafa Gatollari has worked with paranormal investigators on several reality ghost-hunting television shows and has peeked behind the paranormal curtain. "I've also

> "If [ghost-hunting television shows] play the right few seconds of footage any number of times and edit the sequence properly, they could convince just about anyone [of the existence of the paranormal]."[56]
>
> —Brooks Vernon, filmmaker

seen how people intentionally fake evidence of the paranormal—and how they utilize devices that are, to put it bluntly, not worth the plastic they're 3D-printed with," he says. For example, many shows use a REM pod—a device that detects changes in electromagnetic fields—to communicate with ghosts. "There's a slight problem, however—and it's that REM pods are utterly useless for TV purposes,"[57] says Gatollari. REM pods are very sensitive to radio frequencies and cellular communications. In a room filled with a television production crew, microphones, and cell phones, it is impossible to say that any REM pod activity is caused by paranormal activity. Gatollari explains:

> In fact, REM pods can even be triggered at will—and from quite a far distance away, depending on the model—by the simple pressing of a key on a walkie-talkie. I've been to events and investigations where some people, presumably because they get a kick out of scaring folks, intentionally fake REM pod interactions by keying walkies to make it seem like there's "something strange in your neighborhood."[58]

Ghost-Hunting Communities

Whether real or fake, ghost hunting on small and large screens has captivated audiences and helped build a community of interest. People fascinated by paranormal investigations can connect through in-person meetings, events, and conventions. Many also share paranormal interests and experiences online through internet forums, social media sites, and websites.

In Sault Ste. Marie, Michigan, paranormal enthusiasts gather for the Michigan Paranormal Convention (MIPARACON). Held annually since 2009, the convention is hosted by the Upper Peninsula Paranormal Research Society. Over several days, the convention features paranormal experts, television stars, and other speakers who share stories about the paranormal world. "Humans have

Living for the Dead

Premiering in 2023, *Living for the Dead* was the first paranormal investigation television show to feature five LGBTQ ghost hunters. The show is narrated by actor Kristen Stewart as the five queer ghost hunters travel across the United States to investigate reported paranormal activity. Ken Boggle reads tarot cards, while Juju Bae is a practicing witch. Logan Taylor is the team's psychic medium, and Alex LeMay works as its technical expert. Roz Hernandez is the team's lead paranormal investigator. Together, they work to help the living and dead communicate and coexist in peace. "A lot of times, these paranormal shows will provoke a spirit in order to get a response," says Rob Eric, who is the show's executive producer along with Stewart. "I think what our team did so beautifully was not provoke the spirit, but actually try to understand what's going on. Why is the situation happening? Because at the end of the day you're there to help somebody else," he says.

Quoted in Gina Sirico, "Queer Ghost-Hunters Investigate the Paranormal in Hulu's *Living for the Dead*," ABC 7 Chicago, October 18, 2023. https://abc7chicago.com.

always been attracted to what falls out of the realm of everyday explanation. People are fulfilled and entertained when they delve into inexplicable phenomena with a critical eye. Especially with others who have the same interest. Exploring things outside the normal has come to define a lifestyle," says convention organizer Brad Blair. Some of the biggest highlights of the convention are the panel discussions in which paranormal experts and celebrities talk about what is new in the paranormal world. "People get a real rush talking with someone who investigates mysterious things for a living. They get a picture or autograph with a favorite author or TV personality. There's a chance to personally ask direct questions and even give feedback. That in itself is worth the expense of traveling to MIPARACON,"[59] says Blair.

Many websites, online forums, discussion groups, and social media groups connect paranormal investigators, researchers, and enthusiasts worldwide. They share tips about paranormal equipment, insight into haunted locations, and firsthand experiences with paranormal investigations. Some websites even offer online classes in paranormal investigations, in which students learn how to conduct a detailed, ethical, and legal paranormal investigation of a potentially haunted site.

Searching for Answers

Throughout history, humans have been fascinated by what happens after death and the idea of spirits of the dead that can communicate with the living. According to Eddy White, a humanities professor at the University of Arizona, that attraction to the paranormal is part of a common human impulse to a search for meaning in a complicated world. "There seems to be a certain degree of randomness and chaos to the lives we lead, and sometimes people want structure or explanations to human existence," says White. "Paranormal or supernatural phenomena can help provide that meaning." Also, as fewer Americans participate in organized religion, especially young people, belief in the supernatural is rising. "For some younger people, organized religions are not appealing or are not able to provide answers that are compelling or make sense to them. So they look for answers elsewhere,"[60] says White.

> "There seems to be a certain degree of randomness and chaos to the lives we lead, and sometimes people want structure or explanations to human existence. Paranormal or supernatural phenomena can help provide that meaning."[60]
>
> —Eddy White, professor of humanities at the University of Arizona

Jerry Hogle, a professor of English at the University of Arizona, has a more straightforward explanation for the popularity of ghosts and the paranormal: being scared is fun. Hogle points out that when people are scared but not truly in danger, hormones in the body called endorphins rise, which improves mood. "We're in a state of heightened awareness, but we know at the same time that we are safe. We can take pleasure in the endorphins going off like this without actually being threatened,"[61] says Hogle. Curiosity and excitement over confronting the unknown will continue to attract many more people to the intriguing tales of ghost hunting.

Introduction: Searching for Spirits

1. Quoted in Dan McGowan, "One of the World's Most Famous Ghost Hunters Lives in Rhode Island—and She's Got Stories to Tell," *Boston Globe*, October 29, 2020. www.bostonglobe.com.
2. Quoted in Kelly Skye Fadroski, "'Kindred Spirits' Host Amy Bruni Explains How to Talk to Ghosts, and Shares a Queen Mary Scare in New Book," *Los Angeles Daily News*, October 21, 2020. www.dailynews.com.
3. Quoted in Mike Spohr, "Spine-Chilling Stories: Nurses Recall Ghostly Encounters and Supernatural Experiences While On Duty," BuzzFeed, May 2, 2024. www.buzzfeed.com.
4. Quoted in Emily Glimco, "Interview with a Ghost Hunter: Addison Resident to Share Tales of the Paranormal at the Library," *Arlington Heights (IL) Daily Herald*, September 30, 2021. www.dailyherald.com.

Chapter One: The World of Ghost Hunting

5. Quoted in Science History Institute, "Ghost Hunting in the 19th Century," July 6, 2021. www.sciencehistory.org.
6. Quoted in Houghton Library, "Psychical Research," 2023. https://library.harvard.edu.
7. Quoted in Science History Institute, "Ghost Hunting in the 19th Century."
8. Quoted in Beth Braden, "Amityville: Inside the Case That Rattled a Seasoned Paranormal Investigator," Travel Channel, 2024. www.travelchannel.com.
9. Quoted in Katherine Mansfield, "Whispering Souls Offers Paranormal Experiences to Those with 'an Open Mind,'" *The Almanac*, October 28, 2023. www.thealmanac.net.

Chapter Two: Ghost-Hunting Teams and Tools

10. Quoted in Dierdre Reilly, "Do You See Ghosts in This Video? Vermont Paranormal Investigators Reveal Their Findings," Fox News, October 29, 2022. www.foxnews.com.
11. Quoted in Lex Merrell, "Your Local Ghost Hunters: Paranormal Investigators of New England," *Bennington (VT) Banner*, July 21, 2022. www.benningtonbanner.com.
12. Quoted in University of Warwick, "Ghost Hunting Equipment: What You Need to Know According to an Electricity Expert," 2024. https://warwick.ac.uk.
13. Quoted in Reilly, "Do You See Ghosts in this Video?"
14. Quoted in Meg Leonard, "Spirit Moves Ghost Hunter to Unearth Paranormal Stories," *Grosse Pointe (MI) News*, October 19, 2022. www.grossepointenews.com.
15. MacKenzie Koncher, "I Work in Insurance by Day and Hunt Ghosts by Night. People Think It Must Be Scary—but Investigating the Paranormal Isn't Always What You See on TV," Business Insider, October 28, 2022. www.businessinsider.com.

16. Quoted in Ashley Lewis, "How to Become a Real-Life Ghost Hunter, According to Paranormal Investigators," *Reader's Digest*, December 16, 2022. www.rd.com.
17. Katrina Weidman, "My Story," Katrina Weidman personal website, 2024. www.katrinaweidman.com.
18. Quoted in Andrew DaRosa, "CT Paranormal Researcher Dishes Truth on 'Ghost Hunting,'" CTPost, October 31, 2019. www.ctpost.com.
19. Quoted in DaRosa, "CT Paranormal Researcher Dishes Truth on 'Ghost Hunting.'"
20. Quoted in Tim Leininger, "Paranormal Investigators, Family Say Presence of 7-Year-Old Is in Somers Home," Yahoo! News, October 23, 2021. www.yahoo.com.

Chapter Three: A Night in the Field

21. Quoted in Tim Elliott, "Ghost Hunters Investigate Claims of Spirits Haunting an Old Building in Downtown Sun Prairie," WMTV 15 News, October 30, 2020. www.wmtv15news.com.
22. Quoted in Sam Watson, "Ghost Encounters Increased During Pandemic, Paranormal Investigation Group Says," Madison Commons, March 30, 2022. www.madisoncommons.org.
23. Quoted in Elliott, "Ghost Hunters Investigate Claims of Spirits Haunting an Old Building in Downtown Sun Prairie."
24. Quoted in Glimco, "Interview with a Ghost Hunter."
25. Quoted in Elliott, "Ghost Hunters Investigate Claims of Spirits Haunting an Old Building in Downtown Sun Prairie."
26. Quoted in Bobby Forand, "The Paranormal Investigators," *Motif*, October 10, 2023. www.motifri.com.
27. Forand, "The Paranormal Investigators."
28. Quoted in Lauren Talarico, "Sugar Land PD Cracking Down on Trespassers Breaking Into Historic Abandoned Prison," KHOU-11, November 16, 2021. www.khou.com.
29. Quoted in Lewis, "How to Become a Real-Life Ghost Hunter, According to Paranormal Investigators."
30. Quoted in Jack Sheedy, "Paranormal Investigation Brings Team to Winsted," *New Haven (CT) Register Citizen*, January 2, 2024. www.registercitizen.com.
31. Quoted in Sheedy, "Paranormal Investigation Brings Team to Winsted."
32. Quoted in Sheedy, "Paranormal Investigation Brings Team to Winsted."
33. Quoted in Sheedy, "Paranormal Investigation Brings Team to Winsted."
34. Quoted in Watson, "Ghost Encounters Increased During Pandemic, Paranormal Investigation Group Says."
35. Quoted in Abigail Morici, "An Interview with a Ghost Hunter," *Memphis (TN) Flyer*, October 28, 2022. www.memphisflyer.com.
36. Quoted in Shayna Murphy, "11 Secrets of Paranormal Investigators," *Mental Floss*, October 14, 2022. www.mentalfloss.com.
37. Quoted in Murphy, "11 Secrets of Paranormal Investigators."

Chapter Four: Ghost Hunting: Science or Pseudoscience?

38. Quoted in Jonah Beleckis, "Many Ghost Hunters See Their Work as a 'Pioneering Scientific Effort,' Wisconsin Author Explains," Wisconsin Public Radio, October 30, 2023. www.wpr.org.
39. *Encyclopaedia Britannica*, "Science," July 11, 2024. www.britannica.com.
40. Quoted in Beleckis, "Many Ghost Hunters See Their Work as a 'Pioneering Scientific Effort,' Wisconsin Author Explains."
41. Bruce Greyson, "'I Study NDEs. What I've Learned About Near-Death Experiences Changed My Life,'" *Newsweek*, March 13, 2021. www.newsweek.com.
42. Greyson, "'I Study NDEs.'"
43. Quoted in Liza, "Podcast with Transcript (Ep. 5): The Quest (and Challenge) of Psi Research," Mindstream, March 15, 2020. https://mindstreamconnect.com.
44. Quoted in Stephen C. George, "Ghost Busted: When Science Meets the Supernatural," *Discover*, October 7, 2021. www.discovermagazine.com.
45. Quoted in George, "Ghost Busted."
46. Quoted in George, "Ghost Busted."
47. Quoted in George, "Ghost Busted."
48. Benjamin Radford, "The Shady Science of Ghost Hunting," Live Science, October 21, 2022. www.livescience.com.
49. Radford, "The Shady Science of Ghost Hunting."
50. Quoted in Robert Lea, "Paranormal Investigators Who Use Science Reveal What Ghost Hunters Get Wrong," *Newsweek*, October 31, 2021. www.newsweek.com.
51. Quoted in Lea, "Paranormal Investigators Who Use Science Reveal What Ghost Hunters Get Wrong."
52. Kenny Biddle, "Investigating Ghosts at the Knickerbocker Hotel," *Skeptical Inquirer*, June 11, 2024. https://skepticalinquirer.org.

Chapter Five: Ghost Hunting Meets Pop Culture

53. Rae Alexandra, "'Living for the Dead' Is the LGBT Ghost-Hunting Show We Didn't Know We Needed," KQED, October 19, 2023. www.kqed.org.
54. Quoted in Lorraine Ali, "The Comedy Store Is Rumored to Be Haunted. So We Went Ghost Hunting with the Pros," *Los Angeles Times*, October 28, 2022. www.latimes.com.
55. Brooks Vernon, "Are Ghost-Hunting Shows Real or Fake? Paranormal TV Tricks Explained," Screen Rant, July 18, 2021. www.screenrant.com.
56. Vernon, "Are Ghost-Hunting Shows Real or Fake?"
57. Mustafa Gatollari, "I've 'Hunted Ghosts' for Paranormal TV Shows My Whole Career. These Are the Tricks They Use to Fool You," *The Independent* (London), August 12, 2022. www.independent.co.uk.
58. Gatollari, "I've 'Hunted Ghosts' for Paranormal TV Shows My Whole Career."
59. Quoted in John Shibley, "Stranger Things: Paranormal Convention Attracts Huge Crowd," Soo Leader, August 27, 2022. www.sooleader.com.
60. Quoted in Andy Ober, "Experts Explain Our Love of Fear and Fascination with the Supernatural," University of Arizona, October 25, 2022. https://news.arizona.edu.
61. Quoted in Ober, "Experts Explain Our Love of Fear and Fascination with the Supernatural."

Books

Amy Bruni, *Life with the Afterlife: 13 Truths I Learned About Ghosts*. New York: Grand Central, 2020.

Amy Bruni and Adam Berry, *Ghost Hunting: Scariest Encounters*. New York: Dotdash Meredith, 2023.

Kerrie Logan Hollihan, *Ghosts Unveiled! (Creepy and True #2)*. New York: Abrams, 2020.

Hal Marcovitz, *Teen Guide to the Supernatural*. San Diego, CA: ReferencePoint, 2024.

Michael Teitelbaum, *Famous Ghosts*. Parker, CO: Stride, 2022.

Internet Sources

Lorraine Ali, "The Comedy Store Is Rumored to Be Haunted. So We Went Ghost Hunting with the Pros," *Los Angeles Times*, October 28, 2022. www.latimes.com.

Ashley Lewis, "How to Become a Real-Life Ghost Hunter, According to Paranormal Investigators," *Reader's Digest*, December 16, 2022. www.rd.com.

Benjamin Radford, "The Shady Science of Ghost Hunting," Live Science, October 21, 2022. www.livescience.com.

Science History Institute, "Ghost Hunting in the 19th Century," July 6, 2021. www.sciencehistory.org.

Jack Sheedy, "Paranormal Investigation Brings Team to Winsted," *New Haven (CT) Register Citizen*, January 2, 2024. www.registercitizen.com.

Websites

Atlantic Paranormal Society
htts://the-atlantic-paranormal-society.com
The Atlantic Paranormal Society is a group of ghost hunters who investigate hauntings and other paranormal activity. Their work is featured on the television show *Ghost Hunters*.

Eastern Connecticut Paranormal Society
www.easternctparanormal.com
The Eastern Connecticut Paranormal Society is a team of paranormal investigators who investigate reported hauntings and other paranormal

activity. The group's website features information about recent cases as well as news articles.

Ghost Guild, Inc.
https://theghostguild.weebly.com
The Ghost Guild, Inc. is a nonprofit organization composed of a team of volunteers with a love for history, science, and the unexplained. The group conducts science-based investigations of locations with historical meaning. Its website has links to news articles, information about investigations, and more.

Ghost Research Society
www.ghostresearch.org
The Ghost Research Society investigates ghosts, hauntings, and the paranormal. Its website features information about the society's latest work.

Skeptical Inquirer
https://skepticalinquirer.org
Skeptical Inquirer is a bimonthly magazine published by the Committee for Skeptical Inquiry, an organization with the primary mission of using science to debunk claims of the paranormal and other extraordinary claims. Its website features articles from current and past issues.

Note: Boldface page numbers indicate illustrations.

Act Against Conjuration, Witchcraft, and Dealing with Evil and Wicked Spirits (Great Britain, 1603), 9
Alexandra, Rae, 48
American Society for Psychical Research (ASPR), 12
Amityville Horror, The (film), 49–50
Amityville (NY) haunting, 16–17
Antoniou, Marina, 22
Asimov, Isaac, 43
Atlantic Paranormal Society, 60

Bae, Juju, 55
Bertram, Jason, 29–30, 34
Bible, 9
Biddle, Kenny, 44–46
Blair, Brad, 54–55
Boggle, Ken, 55
Borley Rectory (Essex, England), 15
Bray, David, 27, 28
Brujitske, Jen, 24, 25
Bruni, Amy, 5–7, 50

Chick, Theresa, 19
clairvoyance, 39
Committee for Skeptical Inquiry, 43
communication with dead
Judeo-Christian view on, 9
prevalence of belief in, **4**
skepticism about, 13–14
spiritualism movement and, 9–12
Conan Doyle, Arthur, 15
Conjuring, The (film), 49, 51, **51**

D'Agostino, Thomas, 30–31
DeFeo, Ronald, Jr., 16, **17**
digital audio recorder(s), 23, **26**
Division of Perceptual Studies (DOPS, University of Virginia), 39
dowsing rods, 22, 25
Drago, Elisabeth Berry, 11

Eastern Connecticut Paranormal Society (ECPS), 27, 60–61
Eaton, Marc, 37
electromagnetic detectors, 22, 54
extrasensory perception, 39

Faraday, Michael, 13–14
Fox sisters (Maggie, Kate), **10**, 10–11
Freund, Eli, 32, 33, 34

Gatollari, Mustafa, 53–54
Ghost Guild, Inc., 61
ghost hunter(s)
communities of, 54–56
paths to becoming, 25–27
Ghost Hunters (TV program), 5, **6**, 47–49, **48**
ghost-hunting teams, 20–21
equipment used by, 21–25, **26**, **35**, **38**
forming, 27

See also paranormal investigations

Ghost Research Society, 61

Gonsalves, Steve, 50

Greyson, Bruce, 40–41

Haunting of Hill House, The (Jackson), 50

hauntings
residual *vs.* intelligent, 34

Hawes, Jason, 48, **48**

Henderson, Patty, 18

Hernandez, Roz, 55

History of Spiritualism, The (Doyle), 15

Hogle, Jerry, 56

hokey pokey boxes, 24

Hope, William, 14

Houdini, Bess, 13

Houdini, Harry, 13

Hyman, Ray, 43

intelligent hauntings, 34

Jackson, Shirley, 50

James, William, 12–13

Kestrel meters, **38**, 38–39

Knickerbocker, Peg, 46

Knickerbocker Hotel (Linesville, PA), 46

Koestler Parapsychology Unit (University of Edinburgh), 41

Koncher, MacKenzie, 25

Kruth, John, 26

Lamson, Pamela, 28

Land of Mists, The (Doyle), 15

Lara, Pete, 31–32

Leigh, Noah, 41–43

LeMay, Alex, 55

Living for the Dead (TV program), 55

Lutz, George, 16

MacNeil, Ellen, 33, 36

Michigan Paranormal Convention (MIPARACON), 54–55

Miller, Betty, 19

National Laboratory of Psychical Research, 14

near-death experiences, 40

Nichols, Andrew, 52

night vision cameras, 24

O'Connor, Chris, 27, 28

Old Testament, 9

opinion polls. *See* surveys

Ouija boards, 11

out-of-body experiences, 39

paranormal investigations
in books, 50
equipment used by, 21–25, **26**, **35, 38**
field visits, 32–35
in movies, 49–51
no-payment rule for, 33
preliminary interviews in, 29–30
preparing for site visits, 31–32
research in, 30–31
reviewing findings, 35–36
as scientific endeavor, 37–38
TV portrayal of, 36, 47–49

Paranormal Investigators of Milwaukee (PIM), 41–42

Paranormal Investigators of New England (PI-NE), 19

paranormal/paranormal phenomena
historical fascination with, 9, 56
researching, 39–41

searching for alternative explanations for, 43, 44–46

Paranormal State (TV program), 47

parapsychology, 39

Pew Research Center, 7

Pinkey, Stephanie, 34

Piper, Leonora, 12

polls. *See* surveys

Poltergeist (film), 5, 49

precognition, 39

Price, Harry, 14–15

psi, 39

Radford, Benjamin, 44

rationalism, 10

RealClear Opinion Research, 7

reincarnation
prevalence of belief in, **4**

REM pods, 54

residual hauntings, 34

Rhine, Joseph Banks, 39

Sagan, Carl, 43

scientific method, 42

séances, 11–13, **12**

Skeptical Inquirer (journal), 43, 61

skepticism
about communication with dead, 13–14
about ghost hunting, 43–44
role of, in paranormal investigations, 37

Society for Psychical Research, 14

Spielberg, Steven, 50

spirit boxes, 24–25, 33–34

spirits/spirit world
prevalence of belief in, **4**, 7

spiritualism movement, 9–11
in US, 11–12

Stevens, Lindsay, 20–21

Stewart, Kristen, 55

surveys
on belief in ghosts, 7
on belief in spirits/spirit world, **4**

Szabelski, Tony, 8, 30

Taylor, Logan, 55

telekinesis, 39

telepathy, 39

Vandesteeg, Tanya, 35

Vernon, Brooks, 53

Von Klopp, John, 29

Von Klopp, Renee, 29, 35

Warren, Ed, 16–17, 51

Warren, Lorraine, 16–17, 51

Watt, Caroline, 41

Weidman, Katrina, 26–27

Whispering Souls Paranormal Investigations, 18

White, Eddy, 56

Wilson, Grant, 48, **48**